books designed with giving in mind

Bread Baking
The Crockery Pot Cookbook
Kid's Garden Book
Classic Greek Cooking
The Compleat American
      Housewife 1776
Low Carbohydrate Cookbook
The World In One Meal
Kid's Cookbook
Italian
First Brandy Cookbook

Cheese Guide & Cookbook
Miller's German
Quiche & Souffle
To My Daughter, With Love
Natural Foods
Chinese Vegetarian
Four Seasons Party Book
Jewish Gourmet
Working Couples
Paris...and then some
Sunday Breakfast

Fisherman's Wharf Cookbook
Charcoal
Ice Cream Cookbook
Hippo Hamburger
Blender Cookbook
The Wok, a Chinese Cookbook
Christmas Cookbook
Cast Iron Cookbook
Japanese Country
Fondue

from nitty gritty productions

DEDICATION AND ACKNOWLEDGMENTS:

We respectfully dedicate this book to the heroic people of rural Mexico.

We express our sincere appreciation to the many people who have helped us in understanding and appreciating Mexico, and in gathering the material for this book.

We are particularly indebted to Dr. and Mrs. Marvin Peterson and Sr. and Sra. Alfredo Martinez of Mexico City for their wholehearted interest and invaluable assistance.

We are thankful to our conscientious and delightful 12-year-old daughter, Jeanie, for her perfect companionship.

And most of all we are grateful to mother, Mrs. Emily Wallace, without whose help many of our trips to Mexico would have been impossible.

THE AUTHORS

In addition to sheer
gastronomic adventure
and enjoyment,
it is our hope that
our favorite Mexican
recipes (adapted
for the American kitchen
and the photographs
of friends and events
encountered during
our travels there,
convey something of the
feeling of Mexico
as it has been our good
fortune to experience it.

THE MEXICAN COOK BOOK

by George and Inger Wallace

A Nitty Gritty Book*
Published by
Nitty Gritty Productions
P.O. Box 5457
Concord, California 94524

*Nitty Gritty Books — Trademark
Owned by Nitty Gritty Productions
Concord, California

ISBN 0-911954-16-3

CONTENIDO   CONTENTS

FOREWORD

During the past forty years, we have travelled throughout Mexico, seeking to know its people, delighting in the discovery of modern customs that are related to the past. And, inevitably, we have found in the cuisine of Mexico a reflection of a fascinating part of its history.

Mexico's cuisine is a result not only of her own products and people, but the influence of her conquerors: First, the Spanish Conquistadores, who landed on the shores of this country in 1519, made a major impact on its cuisine. They introduced cattle, sheep, pigs, chickens, olives, grapes, rice, wheat, sugar, and cinnamon to Mexico, as well as new herbs and spices — all the flavors of the Orient, the Mediterranean, and the near East. For the next 400 years, chefs and cooks in the convents, monasteries, and mansions of the wealthy in Mexico vied in their attempts to please the increasingly discerning and demanding appetites of their superiors and lords.

Then on September 16, 1810, in a small village in the state of Cuanajuato, Padre Hildalgo y Castillo cried out to his impoverished native flock "Long live the Virgin of Guadalupe! Death to the "gachupines"*!" - and thus signaled the end of domination from Sapin, and the beginning of a courtship of everything French. Today, Mexican cuisine, a composite of all three, is uniquely flavorful, unforgettable, and almost addictive.

It is this diverse, delightful, and exciting cuisine which reflects the freedom of new Mexico we have been experiencing on our trips into the country that we think of as a second home; and it is our treasure trove of recipes and photographs collected from our travels in that country of contrasts which we wish to share with you.

*derogatory expression for Spaniards born in Spain

Entremeses came to colonial Mexico from Spain, where varieties of snacks of every description were served in the hours between dusk and the late, late meal.

Then, as Paris replaced Madrid as the cultural mecca for 19th-century Mexico's social elite, entremeses were replaced by canapes and hors d'oeuvres. Then came the Revolution of 1910, and such foreign influence became passe.

Now, 60 years later, with a new Mexican elite in control, a newly developed middle class, and a country bustling with industry, commerce, and tourism, the social pattern has again changed with the political pattern: Entremeses, expanded, are back!

1

This is one of three large bands of musicians in Teotitlan del Valle, a Zapotec Indian village in the State of Oaxaca. These bands provide all the music for the local religious festivals and pageants.

Entremeses: anything hand-held that can go with a drink. Here are various assortments of food in this category that are designed to hold off starvation while whetting the appetite. They are always served informally with a variety of drinks.

2

From Spain: Anchovies   From Mexico: Chilled Fruits
               Hard-boiled Eggs   Miniature Empanadas
               Mushrooms   Fresh Vegetables
               Pearl Onions   Gusanos de Maguey (worms!)
               Pickles   Miniature Tacos
               Ripe and Green Olives   Pickled Chiles
               Sardines   Roasted Peanuts
               Sausages   Miniature Tamales
               Seviche   Miniature Tostadas

Be sure to douse the fresh fruits and vegetables with chile powder and lemon!

GUACAMOLE

The classic guacamole, predating the Conquest, was made with avocados, onions, and salt. This variation is excellent as a dip with corn chips, as a garnish to accompany tacos and salads, or as a stuffing for tomatoes.

1 cup avocado, mashed
1/3 cup tomatoes, peeled and chopped
2 t canned jalapeño chiles, chopped
1 T onion, chopped
1 garlic clove, minced
1 t lemon juice
2 t parsley, chopped
Salt and pepper to taste

Mash the avocado with lemon juice to retard discoloration. Then blend well with other ingredients. Serve with corn chips and fresh vegetables.

In French uniforms from the era of Maximilian and Carlotta, and carrying rifles from the Mexican Revolution, the boys of Teotitlan take part in a pageant portraying Cortez' first confrontation with the Aztec emperor, Montezuma.

PATE MICHOACANO

A perfect pate with Sangria: red wine, orange and lemon juice, mixed 8:2:1 - sweetened to taste, and served over ice.

1 pound chicken livers	1/4 t salt
6 T butter	1/8 t pepper
1/2 t vinegar	1/4 cup parsley, chopped
1/4 t nutmeg	Parsley sprigs for garnish

Rinse the livers in cold water, then place them in a saucepan with cold water to cover. Bring to the boil and simmer over low heat 5 minutes. Remove from heat and drain. Blend all ingredients except parsley until pate is smooth.

Mix in the parsley, and pour into a buttered mold. Seal the surface with cool, melted butter. Cool in refrigerator.

Turn out onto a serving plate, decorate with parsley sprigs, and serve with an assortment of crackers.

Try this with a sort of Daiquiri: rum, lemon juice, sugar, and water (mixed 3:2:2:1). Chill well, then blend with ice before serving.

1/4 cup vinegar
1/3 cup salad oil
1/2 t tarragon
1/4 t salt
1 1/2 t lemon juice
1/2 garlic clove, mashed
1/2 pound mushrooms

Put all ingredients but the mushrooms in a jar. Shake well. Add mushrooms and marinate several hours in the refrigerator. Shake occasionally to distribute the flavorings.

These are at their best when freshly made.

These go well with Margaritas (4:1, Tequila to Triple Sec or Cointreau, and a little lime juice) in chilled cocktail glasses rimmed with salt.

1 cup walnuts or almonds	1 pinch oregano
Wine vinegar to cover	1/4 bay leaf
1 onion slice	1 pinch thyme
1 garlic clove	1 pinch marjoram
1 parsley sprig, chopped	1 sprig celery leaves, chopped

Drop nuts into boiling water. Let stand 5 minutes. Peel off skin. Soak nuts in cold water for 24 hours, changing water at least 8 times.

Drain nuts, put them in a jar, and cover with vinegar; add remaining ingredients. Shake well. Refrigerate for a minimum of 4 days.

Use a wooden or plastic spoon to remove only the nuts to be used. Put them in a bowl, pour on a little olive oil; garnish with onion rings, strips of avocado, and Monterey Jack (or a mild white) cheese.

At the day-long festivals
honoring the village
patron saint, the
continuous serving of
mescal, beer, and
fruit to the participants,
officials, and honored
guests, is part of
the ritual that all enjoy.

Seviche is customarily served with bolillos (hard rolls) and beer as a light meal. As an appetizer it goes well with any drink.

1 pound fillet of turbot	3 T olive oil
Lemon juice to cover fish	2 canned green chiles, chopped
1/2 onion, chopped	1/4 t oregano
2 large tomatoes, peeled and chopped	Salt and pepper to taste
3 T cilantro, chopped (or parsley)	2 ripe avocados, diced

Cut fish into small cubes. Place in glass bowl, and cover with lemon juice. Let stand in refrigerator for at least 8 hours. This "cooks" the fish.

Add remaining ingredients, except avocado. Refrigerate for a few hours more.

When ready to serve, stir in avocados and arrange in sherbet glasses if to be served as an appetizer. For use as hors d'oeuvres, spear with toothpicks and set in the midst of an assortment of crackers.

9

Made very small (the size of large marbles), these are excellent hors d'oeuvres. Larger, they can contribute to a buffet or be the meat course for a dinner.

Sauce: 2 cups canned tomatoes
1 garlic clove, minced
1 pinch ground cloves
1 pinch ground cinnamon
2 t sugar
1/2 t salt
1 canned jalapeño chile
1 cup water

Puree all ingredients in the blender, then bring to a boil in a saucepan.

Meatballs: 1 pound ground chuck
1/2 onion, chopped
6 mint leaves, chopped
1 cup parsley, chopped
2 hard-boiled eggs, minced
1/2 t salt
1/2 cup raw rice
2 eggs

Mix ingredients and form into balls. Drop into boiling sauce; simmer 1/2 hour.

Serve hot in a chafing dish, covered with the sauce.

10

For a delicious variation, use cooked shrimp instead of ham.

1/4 lb smoked ham, cut into bite-size pieces
1/4 onion, chopped
1 T salsa jalapeña
2 T lemon juice

Mix ingredients in a serving bowl.
Spear meat with toothpicks. Serve with crackers.

Along with cattle, pigs, sheep, goats, and chickens....soups are part of the Spanish legacy the Mexicans adapted and made their own.

Quickly embellishing upon the import, the Indians created their own variations — adding beans, chiles, squash and corn, tortillas, eggs, meat if they had any, and even, on special occasions, dried fish. In many places sopa became and remains the one regular meal of the day.

Slowly but inexorably, tomatoes, potatoes, eggplant, squash, sweet potatoes, corn, new varieties of beans and chiles, and even avocados of the New World, found their way into the soup pots — and on to the royal kitchens of Europe. And just as inexorably, new recipes came back.

Today, these excellent soups are served family-style from large tureens, providing the first course of the comida, the midday meal.

13

Their work in the fields caught up and the rainy season begun, mestizos from San Juan Chilateca wait for a ride to a nearby fiesta where they will earn extra money as professional musicians.

For a wonderfully rich soup, use cream instead of milk. This is a fabulous soup to precede any elegant entree.

2 cups rich chicken broth
3/4 pound fresh asparagus
2 T butter
2 T flour

1 cup milk
1/2 cup fresh mushrooms, sliced
1 T butter

Cut the asparagus into 2-inch lengths, discarding any tough stems.

Bring broth to a boil, add asparagus, cover the pan, and boil over low heat until asparagus is tender (about 3 minutes).

In another pan, melt the butter, stir in flour, and cook until mixture thickens a little. Add a little broth and bring to a boil, stirring constantly. Slowly add the remaining broth and asparagus, and then the milk. Let the mixture simmer gently.

Saute the mushrooms 2 minutes in butter; add them to soup, and serve.

SOPA DE AGUACATE

Excellent when served hot, this is a zestful pickup when served ice cold on a sweltering day.

2 T onion, minced	1 small tomato, peeled, seeded, and chopped
2 T butter	Salt and pepper to taste
2 T flour	3 avocados
4 cups chicken broth	1/2 cup sour cream

Saute onion in butter. Add flour to form a thick paste. Stir in broth, a little at a time, then add the tomato; salt and pepper to taste. Simmer this mixture while preparing avocados.

Peel avocados, puree them, and stir in sour cream.

Pour soup into bowls, float 3 spoonsful of avocado mixture into each bowl, and serve hot with garlic toast, or cold with sesame crackers.

Like the other women of San Juan, Julia Sanchez Gil is an excellent cook. With the aid of local herbs and spices, and very little meat, she concocts soups and stews—delicou   delicious!

SOPA DE FRIJOLES NEGROS

1 cup dry black beans
8 cups cold water
2 T oil
1 onion, chopped
2 garlic cloves, minced
1/4 t chile pequin, crushed

1 tomato, peeled and seeded
1/2 t oregano
1/2 t salt
1/8 t pepper
2 T sherry
1 pint sour cream

Wash beans; put them in a large saucepan, add water, cover, and cook slowly until almost tender — about 1 1/2 hours.

Saute onions, garlic, and chile in hot oil. Add tomato and cook until onions are transparent. Add to beans in saucepan.

Add oregano, salt and pepper, and stir well. Cover pan; simmer for 1 hour or until beans are tender.

Puree the beans in a blender, then return the mixture to pan; simmer for 5 minutes. Stir in the sherry. Float a large spoonful of sour cream in each bowl.

Serve with garnish of tortillas, avocado slices, and chopped white onion.

1/2 onion, chopped
1 1/2 T oil
2 tomatoes, peeled, seeded, and chopped
2 quarts chicken broth
3 large ears of corn
1/4 pound Monterey Jack cheese, cut into thin strips (or Cheddar cheese)
2 t parsley, minced
Salt and pepper to taste

Saute onion in hot oil, add tomatoes, and cook until onions are transparent. Add the broth, and bring to a boil.

Cut kernels from the cobs, add to soup, and simmer gently 8 minutes.

Strain the broth and put the pulp with a little of the liquid into the blender to liquify. Then return this mixture to the broth.

Reheat the soup, add the cheese and parsley.

Salt and pepper to taste, and serve with hot French bread.

Good at any time, this is a traditional Christmas Eve dish in Mexico.

3 T butter
1/4 cup onion, minced
1 garlic clove, minced
1 T parsley, minced
1 pound canned oysters, with liquid
1 pint sour cream
1 cup milk
Salt and pepper to taste

Saute onion and garlic in butter until the onion is transparent.
Stir in parsley; add oysters (if large, cut in half), and simmer 5 minutes.
Add sour cream, milk, and salt and pepper to taste.
Heat, but DO NOT BOIL. Serve with crackers.

Fortino Velasquez
played clarinet in the
spas of Tehuacan during
the days of Porfirio
Diaz, fought with the
Carranzistas in the
Revolution, and
then returned to
San Juan Chilateca.
There he directs
his 20-piece family band
with inimitable gusto.

CREMA DE PAPAS

Serve with hot French bread and a fresh fruit salad for lunch!

1 1/2 pound potatoes, peeled and diced
2 cups water with 1 bouillon cube
3 slices bacon, fried until crisp
1 large onion, minced
1 stalk celery, chopped
1 T parsley, chopped
1/4 t dry mustard

Salt and pepper to taste
4 cups milk
1/4 cup grated Parmesan cheese
6 green onions, chopped

21

Boil potatoes with water and bouillon cube until tender. Remove from heat and mash the potatoes in the water they were boiled in.

Fry bacon until crisp; saute onion and celery in fat, and drain.

Add remaining ingredients to soup, and bring to a boil.

Serve sprinkled with grated Parmesan cheese and chopped green onions.

This is a festive dish for a festive occasion, to be served from a soup tureen.

2 fresh pork hocks (or pigs' feet)
1 beef marrow bone
1 t salt
1/4 t pepper
3 garlic cloves, minced
2 chicken breasts, cubed

1 pound lean pork, cubed
2 T mild chile powder
2 canned chipotle chiles + 1 T chili sauce or
   2 jalapeño chiles + 1 T smoked barbecue sauce
1 pound canned tomatoes
2 pounds canned hominy

22

Put first 5 ingredients in large pot, cover with water, and bring to a boil. Turn the heat low and simmer gently, covered, for 3 hours.

Add chicken, pork, chiles, and tomatoes, and more water if needed to keep meat covered. Simmer for another 30 minutes.

Remove marrow bone and ham hocks; return lean meat from hocks to the soup. Add hominy and boil for 15 minutes more.

Serve with the following garnish and salsa.

Sauce: 3 T chile pequin (broiled 2 min.) or 2 T red pepper crushed
1/2 cup water
1 cup vinegar
1/4 cup onion, chopped
1/4 t oregano
Liquify ingredients in the blender. Use sparingly — it's hot!

Garnish: Avocado slices
Shredded lettuce
Radish slices
Chopped green onions
Slivers of Monterey Jack cheese (or a soft white cheese)
Toasted tortilla chips

Many men of nearby
Santa Catarina Minas share
work provided by stills
hidden in the remote
barrancas of this
desolate region.
From these stills comes
the best mescal in all Mexico.

CREMA DE JITOMATE

2 pounds fresh tomatoes, peeled and quartered
3 garlic cloves
1 1/2 cups onions, quartered
1 cube butter
2 T flour
1 quart consomme
1 bay leaf
Salt and pepper to taste
1 cup cream (or canned milk)

25

Put tomatoes in blender with garlic and onion; liquify.

Melt butter in large saucepan; add flour, and brown lightly, stirring constantly.

Add tomatoes, consomme, bay leaf, salt and pepper. Simmer 15 minutes. Add cream and heat, but do not boil.

Sprinkle with croutons, and serve steaming hot.

SOPA DE FLOR DE CALABAZA

Here is a soup we discovered in the remote Mixtec region of southern Mexico. Note: Crookneck squash can be used if blossoms are unavailable.

1 ear fresh corn
1 quart chicken broth
2 cups water
Salt and pepper to taste
1 T cilantro, chopped (or 1 T parsley)
1/2 onion, chopped

1 garlic clove, minced
1/2 cup fresh mushrooms, sliced
1/2 pound squash blossoms, chopped
3 T butter
1/2 cup Monterey Jack cheese, cubed
(or a soft white cheese)

26

Grate the corn by slitting kernels down center of each row, and scraping them off with a dull knife. Mix corn, broth, water, salt and pepper, cilantro, and boil until the corn is tender (about 10 minutes). Saute onion, garlic, mushrooms, and squash blossoms (or squash) in butter for 5 minutes; add them to the soup.

Boil soup 5 minutes more; add cheese cubes, and serve.

CONSOME DE POLLO

This soup is excellent, and the chicken can be used for Enchiladas Acapulco, Turnovers with Chicken, or in any recipe that calls for cooked chicken.

1 2-pound chicken, cut into serving pieces
1 1/2 quarts cold water
1 onion, quartered
3 celery stalks with leaves, chopped
3 leeks, chopped
2 garlic cloves
6 peppercorns
1 t salt

Garnish: 1 onion, chopped
1 tomato, chopped
1 jalapeño chile, chopped
Lemon wedges

27

Wash chicken, put in large pot, and bring to the boil. Add next 6 items. Cover, and simmer until meat is tender (about 2 hours). More water may be added as chicken cooks.

Strain the broth, reserve meat. Serve with garnish.

The origin of these unique Mexican dishes is obscure, but it's probably a very good guess that they are of mestizo — Spanish-Amerindian — inspiration, created out of the need to make a filling meal from whatever could be afforded and kept on hand: tortillas, beans, rice, noodles, or bread, and some broth.

Substantial and delicious, dry soups occupy a regular place on comida menus across the land. Served on individual plates just after the soup course, and topped with grated Parmesan or Romano cheese, these dry soups resemble Italian pastas in their use. They can also accompany a main course in lieu of potatoes, rice, or other similar dish.

Largest of all the Indian markets of Mexico, the Oaxaca market is within a day's travel of every conceivable combination of soil, climate, and topography, and therefore features an exotic and great variety of fruits and vegetables throughout the year.

1 T oil for frying onions and garlic
1 onion, sliced
1 garlic clove, minced
1 T olive oil combined with
    3 T butter (for frying bread)
8 slices dry French bread

1 cup tomatoes, peeled
1/4 t salt
1/2 t sugar
2 cups chicken broth
3 eggs, hard-boiled and sliced
1/4 cup Parmesan cheese

30

Saute onion and garlic in hot oil until golden; remove from pan.

In same pan, add oil and butter; fry bread until nicely browned on both sides.

Puree tomatoes, add salt and sugar, and pour over bread in pan. Add cooked onions and broth, and simmer uncovered until broth is absorbed. (Lift mixture with spatula from time to time, to prevent burning.)

Remove to platter, garnish with sliced eggs, sprinkle with cheese, and serve.

SOPA SECA DE HABAS

1/2 onion, chopped
1 garlic clove, minced
1/2 cup ham, diced
2 T olive oil
1 package (10-ounce) frozen lima beans
1/2 cup white wine
1/2 cup water
2 T parsley, minced
Salt and pepper to taste
1/4 cup grated Parmesan cheese

Saute onion, garlic, and ham in hot oil.

Add remaining ingredients, mix well, cover tightly, and simmer until beans are tender (approximately 15 minutes).

Sprinkle with Parmesan cheese, and serve.

Indians and mestizos alike converge on the large Oaxaca market on Saturdays. They come from lonely huts in the hills and nearby villages in the valley to buy, sell and barter; and to enjoy the excitement of the market place.

ARROZ A LA MEXICANA

1 cup rice
1/4 cup cooking oil
1 small onion, chopped
1 garlic clove, minced
1 T parsley, chopped
1 jalapeño chile, minced
2 1/2 cups chicken broth
1 t salt

Fry rice in hot oil with onion and garlic until lightly browned. Drain off oil. Add boiling broth, parsley, chile, and salt. Cover tightly and simmer for 25 minutes without lifting the lid.

Serve with any main dish.

2 cups chicken broth
1 T cilantro, chopped (or 1 T parsley)
6 tortillas, cut into strips
3 T oil
1 onion, chopped
1 garlic clove, minced

1/4 cup tomato sauce
1 T parsley, chopped
1 t mild chile powder
Salt to taste
1/4 cup grated Parmesan cheese

34

Heat broth and put cilantro in to soak.

Fry tortillas lightly in hot oil; drain on paper towels. In the same pan, saute onion and garlic until tender. Add tomato sauce, parsley, and chile powder.

Strain the broth into the mixture, and add salt if needed. Stir in tortilla strips and allow soup to simmer until almost dry; lift from time to time to prevent burning.

Serve dry soup on large platter, sprinkled with Parmesan cheese.

1/2 pound vermicelli

2 T oil

1 onion, minced

2 garlic cloves, minced

1 cup canned tomatoes, drained, chopped

1/4 t sugar

1/4 t oregano

Salt and pepper to taste

2 cups chicken broth

1/2 cup grated Parmesan cheese

Break vermicelli into 2-inch strips, and fry in hot oil, stirring constantly until lightly browned. Remove, leaving as much of the oil in the pan as possible.

Saute minced onion and garlic in the hot oil, then add the tomatoes, sugar, and oregano. Return the vermicelli to the pan, pour in broth, and stir well. Salt and pepper to taste.

Cover pan and cook over low heat for 30 minutes, stirring often to prevent burning. Finish cooking with pan uncovered if there is much liquid left.

Sprinkle generously with Parmesan cheese before serving.

In many homes salad is a regular part of the comida, or lunch, and is served with the meat. It may be a more formal version of the chilled and peeled fresh vegetables offered from carts in the streets, ready for sprinkling with lemon juice and chile powder and eating on the spot — or accompanied with oil and a little vinegar, for use according to taste. Or the salad may be a Spanish dish featuring meats, fish, and vegetables; or simply cooked vegetables and hard-boiled eggs mixed with mayonnaise; or a variation of the tossed green salads that made their way north and are popular with barbecues in California and the American Southwest.

Served on the same plate with a plain meat or fish, or following fancier fare as a course in itself, any of these suggestions enjoyably enhance a Mexican meal.

On Sunday mornings Tarascan women from the islands of Lake Patzcuaro and woodcutters from surrounding hills, congregate in Erongaricuaro to barter as they always have: fish for firewood. No money ever changes hands.

In Mexico this is a traditional dish for the Christmas Eve buffet.

1 head lettuce
3 oranges, peeled and sectioned
1 large, juicy red apple, seeded, diced, and unpeeled
2 firm bananas, sliced
1 cup pineapple chunks
1 cup canned beets, sliced
1/2 cup toasted peanuts, chopped
Seeds of 1 pomegranate (or 4 T cranberries from whole canned cranberry sauce)
French dressing

Fix a bed of shredded lettuce on a festive serving plate. Arrange fruit and beets on the leaves, sprinkle with the pomegranate seeds and nuts, and serve with your favorite French dressing.

38

A favorite for the buffet table, this salad is a perfect complement to ham.

1 pound canned garbanzo beans
2 T onions, minced
2 T parsley, chopped
3 medium carrots, cooked and diced
1/4 cup olive oil
2 T vinegar

Salt and pepper to taste
Lettuce leaves
8 olives, sliced (ripe or green)
2 hard-boiled eggs, quartered
Mayonnaise

Rinse beans in cold water and drain them well. Mix beans, carrots, onions, and parsley, and stir with oil, vinegar, salt and pepper; chill well.

Mound mixture on lettuce leaves and garnish with sliced olives and quartered eggs. Serve with mayonnaise on the side.

Many of the vendors of the open-air markets in Mexico are women. They live in the towns, rather than in the outlying areas, and buy rather than raise the items they sell. All enjoy the art of bargaining, which is a lively combination of conversation, humor, and contest.

ENSALADA DE FRIJOLES

2 cups canned red kidney beans
3 T lemon juice
1/4 cup olive oil
1 T onion, minced
2 T bell pepper, chopped
1/4 cup celery, chopped
1 garlic clove, minced
1/4 t salt
1/2 t tarragon

Mix all ingredients well. Marinate for several hours before serving, stirring occasionally. Delicious served separately or on shredded lettuce.

The ingredients may also be used substituting string beans for kidney beans.

1 red onion, sliced
2 large oranges, sliced
1 large avocado, sliced
Lettuce leaves
French dressing with tarragon leaves to taste

42

Soak onions in salted ice water while you peel and slice the oranges and avocado.

Drain the onion slices, and arrange alternately with the orange and avocado slices on top of the lettuce.

Pour French dressing overall.

Serve with Chili Con Carne or any rich meat dish.

ENSALADA DE PIÑA Y COL

Excellent with any entree, this salad is particularly good with pork.

1 1/2 cups raw cabbage, shredded
1 cup canned pineapple chunks
1/2 cup raisins, softened in 2 T pineapple juice
2 T mayonnaise
2 T sour cream

43

Mix ingredients just before serving, to keep the flavors from blending.

Most popular of the food of Mexico are those snacks collectively termed 'antojitos.' With antecedents predating the Conquest, these were probably created to serve as a light meal at home, or in the fields, or as snacks in the marketplace, or at fiestas — much as the people in rural Mexico still enjoy them today.

Mexico's tacos, tostadas, empanadas, burritos, and quesadillas are inexpensive as well as tasty, filling, and easy to prepare. For a light meal, part of a larger meal, or between-meal snacks, anytime, anywhere, they're popular throughout the Republic

These serve well for luncheon or a light supper, and provide a delicious use for leftovers as well.

This mestiza woman is one of the many independent small businesswomen preparing and selling antojitos in the streets surrounding the huge Oaxaca market.

8 wheat tortillas
1/2 onion, minced
1 T bacon fat
4 cups refried beans
1/4 head lettuce, shredded
1 cup Monterey Jack cheese, shredded (or Cheddar cheese)

1 large tomato, sliced
1 avocado, sliced
8 green onions, chopped
Bottled green taco sauce to taste

46

Put tortillas in ovenproof dish, sprinkle with 1 t water, cover with lid, and heat for 10 minutes in a 300° oven.

Saute onion in bacon fat; add beans, and heat.

Put a large spoonful of beans in the center of each tortilla, top with lettuce, tomato and avocado slices, onions, and cheese.

Pour on taco sauce to taste, and fold the tortilla over the filling, both sides and ends, to enclose it completely. Put burritos in a square pan and heat in a 350° oven for about 10 minutes. Serve immediately.

We first had tortas at a little stand at the University of Mexico. With a cold beer or soda, they make a superb lunch.

4 individual French bread rolls
2 cups warm refried beans
1 1/2 cups cooked chicken, sliced
4 slices ham
4 slices Cheddar cheese
1 large tomato, sliced
1 large avocado, sliced
4 lettuce leaves
Mayonnaise
4 pickled red Jalapeño strips (or cherry peppers)

Cut rolls in half lengthwise and remove the soft center. Spread with beans, then pile on the remaining ingredients. Close the roll and bite in — if you can.

47

*There is nothing
like a really fresh tortilla
made right under a
prospective customer's
nose by a taco vendor.*

You can vary this recipe by adding beans, meat, onion, and/or garlic.

1 1/2 cups Monterey Jack cheese, shredded (or Cheddar cheese)
6 T green chiles, chopped
6 tortillas
Salt
Oil for frying

49

Put 1/4 cup cheese and 1 T chiles on half of each tortilla; sprinkle with salt.

Heat a small amount of oil in a frying pan, and put the tortillas in, one at a time, without folding. Fry for a few seconds.

Fold the tortillas over the filling, pressing the edges together. Fry on both sides until crisp. Drain on paper towel before serving.

Taco means 'wad' - or 'mouthful.' Actually, a taco is just a tortilla wrapped around anything. Here is a simple taco that can be elaborated with one of the fillings on the opposite page.

50

12 tortillas
3 cups lettuce, shredded
1 large tomato, sliced
1 large avocado, sliced

1 cup Cheddar cheese, shredded
1/2 pint sour cream
Pickled chiles to taste
Bottled green taco sauce to taste

Drop tortillas in hot oil, one at a time. After a few seconds turn, fold in half, and fry to desired crispness. Drain on paper towels and keep warm in a low-heat oven. To serve, open each tortilla gently and insert filling. Let each person select his own condiments.

CHICKEN: 2 cups cooked chicken, shredded
           2 T butter
           1 envelope commercial taco flavoring
           2 canned green chiles, diced
           2 green onions, chopped
           1/2 cup tomatoes, peeled and chopped

Mix all ingredients, and saute in butter.   51

BEEF: 1 T cooking oil   2 ounces ripe olives, chopped
           1/2 onion, minced   1 envelope commercial taco flavoring
           1 garlic clove, minced   Salt and pepper to taste
           1 pound ground beef

Saute onions and garlic in oil; add meat, brown well; add other ingredients.

These girls from San Felipe,
a Zapotec village on the outskirts
of Oaxaca, have just finished
a part of their day's work.
Up long before dawn,
they ground corn,
made tortillas, ran barefoot
to market with their wares
loaded in baskets,
and sold the hot, fresh
tortillas to waiting customers.

TOSTADAS

For an informal gathering, arrange ingredients buffet-style, so everyone can make his own tostada. Keep the beans and meat hot!

8 tortillas
Oil for frying
2 cups refried beans
2 cups meat filling (see page 85)
2 cups shredded lettuce
2 sliced tomatoes

1 large sliced avocado
1/2 cup Parmesan cheese
1 pint sour cream
8 ripe olives, sliced
Pickled chile slices

53

Fry tortillas on both sides in hot oil until crisp. Drain on paper towels.

Spread tortillas generously with refried beans, then meat filling; add lettuce, tomato, and avocado. Sprinkle with Parmesan cheese, top with sour cream, and decorate with pickled chile slices and olives.

Here is an excellent opportunity to use leftover meats, fish, and vegetables.

2 cups flour
2 t baking powder
1 t salt
1/2 cup shortening

1/3 cup ice water
Filling (see opposite page)
Oil for frying

54

Sift flour with baking powder and salt, and cut shortening in with a pastry blender. Add water and knead lightly. (Mix filling - see opposite page.)

Divide mixture into 12 balls; roll each into a circle 1/8-inch thick. Put 1 spoonful of filling on half of each circle. Moisten edges of circles with water, fold over the filling, and press the edges together. Press fork tines around the edges.

Bake in 400° oven for 20 minutes, until golden brown.

OR fry in hot oil (300°) until golden, and drain on paper towels. (These are best fried!)

RELLENOS PARA EMPANADAS

SHRIMP:
2/3 cup canned shrimp, minced
8 T Parmesan cheese, grated
3 T pimento, chopped
2 small eggs, lightly beaten

CHICKEN:
1 cup cooked chicken, minced
2/3 cup mild white cheese, shredded (or Cheddar cheese)
3 T canned green chiles, chopped
6 ripe olives, minced
1/8 t oregano
1 garlic clove, minced

SPINACH:
1 cup cooked spinach, chopped
1 cup Cheddar cheese, shredded
8 strips bacon, fried and crumbled
1/4 t nutmeg

Enchilada - literally 'chiled up' - implies that chiles must be involved, and this is the case. Every enchilada also includes one or more tortillas, briefly fried in oil. The variations in sauces, fillings, toppings, and garnishes, and in the way that the enchiladas are folded, rolled, or stacked, produce an appealing array of functional and regional creations, which you can improvise upon as you wish.

'Tamal' means 'patty' in the Aztec language, and tamales are among the oldest and most Indian of all Mexican dishes. In the simplest form they are seasoned dough wrapped in corn husks and steamed. Delicious with bits of meat and sauce folded into the centers, tamales are a traditional fiesta dish, often served in such quantities that they comprise an entire meal. The dough used in making tamales is made from masa harina, a special flour made by the Quaker Oats Company. It is readily available in supermarkets throughout the United States. Masa harina is also the main ingredient in tortillas and the recipe for making them is printed on each masa harina sack.

On their way home from Mass, these women and children had been waiting in a small store for a momentary downpour to pass.

12 tortillas and oil for frying

Sauce: 1 quart chicken broth
6 T mild chile powder
1/4 garlic salt
1/4 t cumin
Salt and pepper to taste
2 T cornstarch in 4 T water
Bring first 5 ingredients to boil.
Add cornstarch, then boil 1 minute.

Filling: 3 cups cooked chicken, shredded
3/4 cup ripe olives, chopped
3/4 cup blanched almonds, sliced
1/2 cup Cheddar cheese, shredded
1/2 cup sauce
Heat ingredients in 2 T butter.
Garnish: 1 cup Cheddar cheese, shredded
1 pint sour cream
6 green onions, chopped

Fry tortillas quickly on both sides in hot oil. Drain and keep warm in a covered casserole. Dip tortillas in hot sauce, put strip of filling across each one, and roll tightly. Place side by side in pan, sprinkle with cheese, and heat in 350° oven 10 minutes. Spoon sauce overall, top with sour cream and chopped onions, serve.

ENCHILADAS DE RES MOLIDA

12 tortillas and oil for frying

Sauce: 1 quart beef broth
      6 T mild chile powder
      1/4 t garlic salt
      1 t cumin
      2 T cornstarch in 4 T water
Bring first 5 ingredients to boil.
Add cornstarch; boil 1 minute.

Filling: 1 onion chopped with 1 garlic clove
1 T oil
1 pound ground chuck
1 can (4 1/2-ounce) ripe olives, chopped
1/2 cup sauce
2 cups Cheddar cheese, shredded (use
  1 cup for filling, 1 cup for topping)

59

Saute onion and garlic in oil until golden, add meat and brown thoroughly. Add remaining ingredients and heat through. Fry tortillas quickly in hot oil, drain, and keep warm in covered casserole.

Dip tortillas in heated sauce. Put filling across each one, roll tightly, and place side by side in pan. Sprinkle with cheese, heat in 350° oven 10 minutes. Spoon heated sauce overall, and serve.

On Good Friday two of our comadres prepared a special and traditional dish. Their separate cooking hut of bamboo and mud, and its dirt floor, is typical of rural kitchens all over Mexico.

12 tortillas and oil for frying

Sauce: 1 quart beef broth
     6 T mild chile powder
     1/4 t garlic salt
     1/4 t cumin
     Salt and pepper to taste
     2 T cornstarch in 4 T water

Filling: 3 cups Cheddar cheese, shredded
     6 green onions, sliced
     12 pitted ripe olives, quartered
     1 1/2 cups sauce
Mix ingredients well.

61

For sauce: Bring first 5 ingredients to a boil. Add cornstarch and boil 1 minute.

Fry tortillas quickly on both sides. Drain on paper towels and keep warm in a covered casserole.

Dip tortillas one by one in heated sauce; put a strip of filling across each tortilla. Roll tightly, then place side by side in pan. Sprinkle with cheddar cheese and heat in 350° oven for 10 minutes. Spoon heated sauce overall and serve.

ENCHILADAS TAPATIAS

3 cups cooked chicken, shredded, heated
6 carrots, peeled and sliced
2 large boiling potatoes, peeled and sliced
1/3 cup Parmesan cheese, grated
8 radishes, sliced
4 romaine lettuce leaves
1 quart enchilada sauce (see page following)

62

Boil carrots and potatoes in salted water until just tender. Drain, fry in hot oil for 1 minute, and keep warm.

Coat each tortilla with sauce, then fry on each side in hot oil; place 1/4 cup of chicken on each tortilla, roll up, and keep warm in ovenproof dish.

Top with carrots and potatoes, sprinkle with cheese, and serve with garnish of radishes and lettuce.

Sauce: 5 ancho chiles (see page 173 for preparation) or 5 T mild chile powder.
1/4 t salt
2 garlic cloves, minced
1/4 onion, minced
2 T cooking oil

Put chiles in a pan, cover with water, add salt. Bring to a boil and let stand 5
minutes.

Puree garlic and onion in blender, add chiles with 1 cup water, (or the chile powder and 1/2 cup water), and blend lightly.

Fry in oil over high heat for 5 minutes, stirring to prevent burning. Lower heat if sauce spatters too much.

Guadalupe and her
mother-in-law,
Asuncion,
remove the seeds
and veins from
dried chiles.
Their plaid skirts
and ribbon-braided
hair are traditional
village dress.

ENCHILADAS HUICHOL

6 tortillas
1 1/2 cups cooked chicken, shredded
1/4 cup oil for frying

Sauce: 1/2 cup sesame seeds, toasted
        1/4 cup water
        1/2 t salt
        1 pinch cumin seeds
        1 T canned jalapeño chile
    Puree ingredients in blender.

Put each tortilla in hot oil, spread with 1 spoonful of sauce, turn, spread spoonful of sauce on other side. Roll up tortillas individually and set aside on warm, covered plate.

Heat the meat in a pan with the remaining sauce, spread mixture over the enchiladas, and serve.

ENCHILADAS SUISAS ROJAS

Red Swiss Enchiladas
Serves 4

12 tortillas and oil for frying

Filling: 1/2 onion, chopped
1 garlic clove, minced
2 T cooking oil
3 cups cooked chicken, shredded
1 cup sauce (see opposite page)
Salt and pepper to taste
1 cup Monterey Jack or Cheddar cheese, shredded

Garnish: 1 cup warm sour cream
6 green onions, chopped

66

Saute onion and garlic in hot oil. Add chicken, brown slightly, stir in sauce and seasoning. Heat, and keep warm.

Fry tortillas quickly in hot oil. Drain and keep warm in casserole. Dip tortillas in heated sauce, put a strip of filling across each, and roll tightly. Arrange side-by-side in pan, sprinkle with cheese, and heat in 350° oven 10 minutes.

Spoon heated sauce over enchiladas and serve with garnish.

Sauce: 8 T mild chile powder
2 canned chipotle chiles + 1 T sauce from can
   or 2 jalapeño chiles + 1 T smoked barbecue sauce
1 onion, quartered
1 garlic clove
1 can (10-ounce) tomato sauce
1 t each: salt, oregano, cumin, sugar
1/8 t pepper
2 T oil
3 cups chicken broth
1 cup half-and-half
2 T cornstarch dissolved in 4 T half-and-half

Puree first 8 ingredients, then fry for 5 minutes in hot oil, stirring constantly.
Add remaining ingredients and simmer for 2 minutes.

With methods as old as
the Conquest itself,
the women of Teotitlan
spin yarn for the
woolen serapes for
which their
village is so famous.

ENCHILADAS POTOSINAS

6 tortillas and oil for frying
1 1/2 cup cooked chicken, shredded
1/2 cup sour cream

Sauce: 2 garlic cloves   2 bell peppers, roasted, peeled, seeded, sliced
       1 onion slice, 1/4-inch thick   1/2 cup water
       1 T jalapeño chiles, minced   1 T olive oil
       1/2 t salt

For sauce: Puree first 6 ingredients, then fry in oil 5 minutes.

Put tortillas in hot oil in frying pan, one at a time; spread with spoonful of sauce, turn over, and spread second side; roll up and set aside on warmed and covered plate. Repeat process for each tortilla.

Heat the meat in a pan with the remaining sauce, spread it over the enchiladas. Serve topped with a spoonful of sour cream.

For these you make the tortillas - it's as easy as making pie dough.

Tortillas: 3 ancho chiles prepared, page 173 (or 3 T chile powder)
1 1/3 cups water
1/2 t salt
2 cups masa harina
1/2 cup Romano cheese, grated

70

Put the chiles in a saucepan with water and salt, and boil 2 minutes. Cool to lukewarm, liquify in blender, and mix with masa and cheese to form a smooth dough. Refrigerate for 1 hour.

Separate dough into 16 balls; flatten each between 2 sheets of wax paper to about 1/8-inch thickness. Peel off paper. Fry tortillas in a lightly greased pan, just until dry.

One by one, dip tortillas in heated sauce and spread with filling. Stack 4 high, top with shredded cheese, and serve.

Sauce: 1 T oil for frying   1/4 t salt
　　　　　1 onion, chopped　　　　　　　　　　　　　2 cups chicken broth
　　　　　4 tomatoes, peeled, seeded, chopped
　　　　　1/2 cup canned green chiles, chopped
　　　　　4 t mild chile powder
　　　　　1/2 t pasilla chile powder (optional)

Saute onion in oil, add next 5 ingredients, and cook 10 minutes.
Puree mixture in blender, add broth, and reheat.

Filling:　1/2 pound chorizo sausage (see page 127)
　　　　　1/2 pound ground beef
　　　　　1 onion, chopped

Fry chorizo, beef, and onion until brown.
Garnish:　1/4 pound Monterey Jack cheese, shredded (or Cheddar cheese)

On her 20th birthday
Juanita is happy
and shy in the new
dress her
husband bought her.
This is the first
time since she was a
child that she has
worn anything
other than
the traditional
dress of her village.

30 corn husks, soaked in hot water 1 hour
4 cups masa harina
1 cup lard

1 t salt
4 t baking powder
3 cups warm meat broth

Beat lard until light and fluffy. Add dry ingredients and beat well. Gradually add broth, beating until mixture is light, and a spoonful dropped in cold water floats. (See page 75 for filling.)

Shake water off corn husks. Spread dough (1/4 inch thick and 4 inches square) near middle of each husk. Put spoonful of filling in center of dough; fold over to seal in filling. Wrap husks around dough and tie ends with string, or fold under.

Stack tamales loosely on rack in steam kettle or covered roasting pan; cover with a folded towel; steam over boiling water without uncovering for about 2 hours. Using heavy mitt or tongs, carefully uncover other tamales as little as possible, and remove one. If dough comes cleanly away from husks, the tamales are done.

73

TAMALES CALIFORNIOS

30 corn husks soaked in hot water 1 hour (or wet parchment)

4 cups cornmeal

1 t salt

1/2 t cumin

4 cups broth

3 T mild chile powder

1 cup Crisco

Bring broth to a boil, add seasonings, and stir in cornmeal. Cook 1 minute, stirring constantly, add Crisco, and stir until well blended. (Filling next page.)

Shake water off corn husks. Spread dough (about 1/4 inch thick and 4 inches square) near the middle of each husk. Put a spoonful of filling in the center of the dough and fold over to seal filling. Wrap husks around dough and tie ends with string or fold under.

Stack tamales loosely on rack in steam kettle or covered roasting pan, cover with a folded towel, and steam over boiling water without uncovering for 1 hour. Using a heavy mitt or tongs, carefully uncover other tamales as little as possible, and remove one. If the dough comes cleanly away from the husk, the tamales are done. (10 min. in pressure cooker = 1 hour in kettle.)

RELLENO DE RES, PARA TAMALES

Beef Tamale Filling
Fills 50

Filling:
2 1/2 pounds lean beef
1 t salt
1 T cumin
1/4 cup mild chile powder
1 onion, chopped
3 garlic cloves, minced
1/8 t cayenne pepper
2 cups beef broth (from meat)
2 T cornstarch dissolved in 4 T broth
2 T pickled red Jalapeño chiles, chopped

Mole Sauce:
6 T butter
6 T flour
1 quart hot meat broth
1/4 t garlic salt
1/4 t cumin
6 T mild chile powder

For Mole Sauce: Melt butter, add flour over low heat, stirring well. Now add broth slowly, still stirring, then seasonings; bring to a boil. Serve with tamales.

Immerse first 7 ingredients in saucepan with water, cover, and simmer until meat is tender. Remove meat, shred it. Mix broth, chiles, and cornstarch; bring to a boil, stirring constantly. Pour mixture over meat. Reserve.

When Cortes and his Spanish Conquistadores sat down to dine with Montezuma, emperor of Mexico, they were offered more than 500 different dishes, many of which contained vegetables they had never seen before. Corn, tomatoes, avocados, and Mexican chiles were a new experience to the Spaniards, some of whom would not touch the tomatoes, thinking they were poisonous.

Then, as now, most Mexican vegetables are rarely cooked alone. Rather they are mixed with various other vegetables, spices, and meats, in a combination where each ingredient complements the other.

We have included here the most popular and available of Mexican vegetable dishes, though should you travel to Mexico you would find a much greater variety as well as many vegetables and herbs you probably would not recognize.

Here, as in other recipes, imagination is the keynote. Don't be afraid to improvise: Let your taste buds be your guide!

The Mixteca, a beautiful region in Mexico when the Conquistadores arrived, is today the most nostalgic. Its hard-working, impoverished mestizos are the legacy the Spanish left behind.

1 pound dry pinto beans
7 cups water
1/4 t cumin
2 garlic cloves, minced
3 T bacon fat
1 t salt
1/2 large onion, minced

Wash beans, removing any loose skins or shriveled beans.

Put beans in a large pot, add water, cumin, and garlic. Cook over low heat for 1 1/2 hours.

Add bacon fat, salt, and onion, and continue cooking until beans are tender — approximately 1 1/2 hours more.

Add more water if beans get too dry. They should be 'soupy.' Stir occasionally to keep them from sticking to the pan. Do not overcook them.

In Mexico these beans are served with practically every meal. By putting a bit of bacon fat in the frying pan, they can be heated over and over again - improving each time.

2 T bacon fat
2 cups cooked Mexican beans
1/2 cup Cheddar cheese, shredded

Heat bacon fat in frying pan. Add beans and a little of the liquid. Mash well.

Fry the beans for a few minutes, turning to prevent burning, until they form a thick paste.

Top with shredded cheese and serve. Cheese may be melted under the broiler, if desired.

With most of the
Mixteca deforested
and eroded,
every slope with
any soil is put to use.
This family
cultivates its hillside
aided by oxen
and a homemade plow.

TORTITAS DE COLIFLOR

Try cooking squash, eggplant, or asparagus this way: Delicious!

1 medium cauliflower
3 large eggs, separated
3 T flour
Salt and pepper to taste
4 ounces Monterey Jack cheese, cubed (or Cheddar cheese)
Oil for frying

Pour boiling water over cauliflower and cook for 20 minutes in an uncovered pan, adding a little salt after 10 minutes.

Separate eggs; beat whites until stiff; beat yolks well and fold into whites. Salt and pepper to taste, then fold in flour.

Break cauliflower into several pieces and insert a cube of cheese in the middle of each. Dip in egg batter, being sure to cover well, and brown in hot oil.

Serve with chile sauce. (See page 83.)

CHILES RELLENOS DE QUESO

8 canned green chiles
8 ounces soft white cheese, cut into strips
3/4 cup refried beans
4 eggs, separated

1 T water
1/4 t salt
4 T flour
Oil for frying

82

Cut a slit in each chile. Insert a spoonful of beans and strips of cheese (the more the better), and close the slit back up.

Beat egg whites until very stiff. Beat egg yolks well with water and salt, and fold them into the whites; now, fold in the flour.

Dip each chile in the batter, then slide it into about 1/2 inch hot oil in a large frying pan. Be sure each chile is well covered with batter. Cover any bare spots with more batter. Turn the chiles right away and continue frying until both sides are a golden brown. Don't crowd them in the pan!

When done, drain on paper towels, serve hot — plain or with sauce and adorned with cheese, as on the following page.

CHILES RELLENOS LUJO

8 stuffed and fried chiles (opposite page)
8 slices mild white or Cheddar cheese

Sauce: 1/2 onion, minced
1 garlic clove, minced
1 T oil
1 cup chicken broth
1 1/2 cups canned tomatoes, chopped

1 T mild chile powder
1/2 t oregano
1/4 t cumin
Salt and pepper to taste

Saute onion and garlic in hot oil, add remaining ingredients; cook 10 minutes.

Place hot stuffed chiles in a shallow pan with raised sides. Put a generous slice of cheese on each chile, pour sauce overall, and heat in 350° oven until cheese is melted.

Serve with refried beans or Mexican rice.

The persistence of the Mixtecs in attempting to eke a living out of weaving hats from palm fronds rather than move off their land, has been referred to as the 'straw-hat sickness.' At eight cents profit per hat, families thus occupied manage somehow to survive.

CHILES RELLENOS DE PICADILLO

Here is an alternate filling for chiles as prepared on page 82.

1/2 pound ground beef
1/2 onion, chopped
1 garlic clove, minced
1 T oil
4 T canned green chiles, chopped
1 cup canned tomatoes, drained

1/4 cup raisins, chopped
1/2 t salt
1/2 t cinnamon
1/8 t oregano
2 T blanched almonds, slivered

85

Brown meat, onion, and garlic in hot oil. Add the remaining ingredients except the nuts, and simmer for 30 minutes. Stir frequently to prevent burning.

Add almonds and cook for a few minutes more.

This filling is also excellent for tostadas and tacos. Freeze it if you like.

Hot buttered ears of 'elote,' sprinkled with chile powder, are among the treats offered in the Mexican markets and streets. Here is another version.

4 ears fresh corn
4 T butter
1/2 cup milk
2 green onions, sliced
4 T bell pepper, chopped
Salt and pepper

86

Slit down the center of each row of corn kernels with a sharp knife, then scrape out the pulp with the dull edge of the knife.

Melt the butter in a saucepan, add milk and corn pulp; cook for 5 minutes, stirring to prevent burning.

Add the onion and bell pepper. Season to taste with salt and pepper. Serve.

PAPAS EN SALSA DE MOSTAZA

2 pounds potatoes
2 T oil
2 T butter
1 1/2 cups chicken broth
1 1/2 T mustard
3 egg yolks, slightly beaten
Salt and pepper to taste
Chopped parsley

Boil potatoes; peel and slice them while still hot.

Heat oil and butter in a frying pan; brown potatoes; keep warm in covered dish when done.

Mix broth, mustard, egg yolks, salt and pepper in frying pan. Add potatoes, and let mixture boil a couple of minutes, stirring constantly.

Sprinkle with parsley and serve.

Living as they do in widely
scattered huts, so deep
in the Mixteca that
they had never seen an
American, these girls
are fortunate in having a
good four-year elementary
school to attend. Here
they enjoy most their
outdoor clothesmaking class.

4 strips bacon
1 medium onion, chopped
1 large tomato, peeled and chopped
1 pound zucchini, unpeeled, sliced
Salt and pepper to taste
1/3 cup Parmesan cheese, grated

Fry bacon until crisp, drain.

Saute onion in 2 T bacon fat until soft. Add tomatoes and zucchini; season to taste. Cover and simmer until zucchini is just tender — about 10 minutes.

Crumble bacon, stir into mixture, sprinkle with Parmesan cheese, place under broiler until brown, and serve.

1 package (10-ounce) frozen, French-cut string beans
2 T onion, minced
1/2 pound fresh mushrooms, sliced
4 T almonds, slivered
1 T olive oil
2 red pimentos, cut into strips
1 T parsley, chopped
1 T butter
Salt and pepper to taste

Cook beans according to directions on package; drain well.
Saute onions, mushrooms, and almonds in hot oil.
Add drained beans, pimentos, parsley, and butter. Heat for a few minutes.
Salt and pepper to taste before serving.

TORTAS DE VERDURAS

Spinach, asparagus, string beans, broccoli, mushrooms, and nopalitos - young cactus leaves (a Mexican favorite), can be cooked this way. For a surprisingly good dish, add a little crisp bacon, cooked shrimp, or crab.

1 pound vegetables, chopped
2 eggs
1/2 cup flour
1 t baking powder
Salt and pepper to taste
Butter

Wash the vegetables in cold water and drain well.

Beat the eggs in a bowl, sift in flour and baking powder. Add the chopped vegetables, salt and pepper, and mix well.

Heat butter in a frying pan, and drop the mixture in by large spoonsful. Fry like pancakes, and serve.

Bordered as it is with over 6000 miles of shoreline, and with her excellent fishing grounds just offshore, Mexico has a tradition of excellent seafood cuisine.

Even at the time of the Conquest, relays of foot runners were delivering fresh fish from the Pacific and the Gulf to Montezuma's court in Tenochtitlan, site of present day Mexico City. Packed in baskets of wet leaves, the fish were kept chilled by the breezes around the leaves as long as the runners kept moving.

To this Spain — drawing not only from lore gleaned from numerous invasions and occupations she had sustained, but also from the cuisine and resources of continental Europe and the Mediterranean basin — made her own rich contributions.

When the olives, oil, onions, and garlic of Spain were added to the natural abundance of Mexico, the groundwork was well laid for the outstanding fish dishes that followed, and which are still popular in Mexico today.

93

Close family relationships are often sustained by traditional family crafts and ancient customs.

ALMEJAS CASA CARLOS

Clams Casa Carlos
Serves 2

Here is an easy and delicious dish from the old Casa Carlos in Chihuahua.

2 pounds clams in the shell
1 1/2 cups boiling water
2 garlic cloves, minced
1/4 cup fresh parsley, chopped

2 T olive oil
1 T cornstarch, dissolved in 2 T cold water
DO NOT ADD SALT

94

Scrub clams well, place in saucepan, and pour boiling water overall. Cover pan tightly, steam for a few minutes — until all shells are open — then remove clams and shells. Strain broth, using a paper towel in the bottom of the strainer to catch any particles. Reserve broth.

Saute the garlic and parsley in hot oil, add the broth, and bring to a boil. Thicken with cornstarch.

Place clams on the half shell in the broth to reheat.

Serve arranged in half shells in soup plates, with broth poured overall.

CAMARONES AL MOJO DE AJO

This elegantly simple dish is as delicious as it is popular in Mexico. The garlic flavor is much milder than expected.

2 T oil
2 T butter
8 garlic cloves, chopped
1 pound raw prawns, shelled (or large shrimp)
Salt and pepper to taste
Lemon wedges

Heat oil and butter in a large frying pan.

Add garlic, then prawns, in a single layer. Sprinkle with salt and pepper. Fry only until prawns have turned pink (3 or 4 minutes), then fry other side.

Serve with lemon or lime wedges.

Jose is one of the countless shoeshine boys in Mexico who supplement the family income by their earnings. Here he is polishing up his sister's carefully kept shoes for a village fiesta.

HUACHINANGO A LA VERACRUZANA

Here is the best known and most popular of all fish dishes in Mexico.

1 pound fillets of red snapper
2 T oil for frying
1/2 cup onion, chopped
2 garlic cloves, minced
1 can (1-pound) tomatoes, drained
3 T parsley, chopped
1 T vinegar
1 t salt

1 bay leaf
1/4 t each: thyme, marjoram, oregano
1 t sugar
1/4 cup water
9 stuffed green olives, sliced
2 t capers
1 canned green chile, chopped
2 T olive oil

Rub fish with lemon, sprinkle with salt and pepper. Fry 1 minute on each side in hot oil; remove to a baking dish. Saute onion, garlic, and tomatoes in remaining oil for 5 minutes; add next 9 ingredients; cook 2 minutes more.

Top fish with olives, capers, and chiles; pour sauce overall; drizzle with oil, and bake in 300° oven until fish flakes apart (about 30 minutes).

Of Spanish origin, paella is a real fiesta dish - a whole meal in itself.

3 T cooking oil
1/2 pound lean pork, cubed
1 chicken breast, cubed
1/2 cup ham, cubed
3 strips bacon, quartered
8 artichoke hearts
2 large tomatoes, peeled and quartered
3 garlic cloves
3 canned chipotle chiles (or 3 jalapeño chiles + 3 T smoked barbecue sauce)
1/2 onion, diced
1/2 cup chorizo sausage, rolled into small balls
1/4 pound raw shrimp, peeled
8 claims in the shell
1/2 cup crab, in chunks

1 cup frozen peas

1 cup frozen string beans

1 stalk celery, chopped

1/2 t saffron

2 cups rice

4 cups boiling water mixed with 1 t salt

4 hard-boiled eggs, halved

8 ripe olives, sliced

1/3 cup parsley, chopped

1 small can pimentos, cut into strips

Brown the pork, ham, chicken, bacon, and artichoke hearts in hot oil, then put them in a large stewing pot.

Puree the tomatoes, garlic, chiles, and onion in a blender for 1 minute; strain to remove the seeds. Fry mixture in hot oil for 5 minutes, then pour over meat.

Fry the chorizo in a separate pan; discard fat and add the meat to the pot. Then add the seafood, vegetables, rice, and the boiling water with saffron in it.

Cover the pot tightly. Steam contents over low heat 30 minutes or until the rice is tender.

Arrange paella on a large serving platter. Garnish with the eggs, olives, and parsley. Decorate with pimento strips.

This vanilla bean farmer
in Papantla, on the
hot and humid Gulf Coast,
prefers traditional
Totonac dress
for himself, but indulges
in factory-made
clothes for his children.

PESCADO A LA MADELENE

1 1/2 pounds fillets of turbot, red snapper, bass, or halibut
1/3 cup almonds
1/2 cup parsley
2 T butter, melted
2 t lemon juice
Salt and pepper to taste

Chop almonds and parsley together. (This helps blend the flavors and keeps the almonds from getting all over the kitchen.)

Put fish in a baking dish and sprinkle with the almond-parsley mixture.

Mix butter and lemon juice; pour half of mixture over fish. Sprinkle fish with salt and pepper, cover tightly with foil, and bake in 350° oven for 15 minutes.

Unwrap fish, pour rest of butter-lemon mixture overall, and bake uncovered for another 10 minutes.

Serve with lemon wedges.

3 T oil
1 large onion, chopped
1 garlic clove, minced
1 pound fresh tomatoes, peeled and sliced
1 pound shrimp, raw or cooked, shelled
1/4 cup parsley, chopped
1 T capers
1/3 cup Spanish olives
Salt and pepper to taste

102

Saute onion and garlic in hot oil. Add tomatoes and simmer 2 minutes. Add shrimp, parsley, capers, and olives. Sprinkle with salt and pepper, and simmer until almost dry (about 30 minutes).

Serve with hot buttered French bread.

CAMARONES CON ARROZ

This popular dish can also be made with lobster, crawfish, or crab - or use a combination, if you like. In many homes whatever is seasonal is used.

2 small onions, chopped
2 garlic cloves, minced
1/4 cup olive oil
1/2 green bell pepper, chopped
1 large tomato, peeled and diced
1 pound large raw shrimp, peeled
3/4 cup white wine

3 cups chicken broth
1/2 t freshly-ground pepper
1/8 t basil
1/2 t salt
2 cups rice
1/3 cup grated Parmesan cheese

103

Saute onion and garlic in hot oil until onion is transparent. Add bell pepper and shrimp, and cook until shrimp turn pink.

Add remaining ingredients EXCEPT rice, mix well, and bring to a boil.

Now stir in rice, cover pan, and cook over medium heat for 25 minutes. Sprinkle with Parmesan cheese, and serve.

Bountiful as nature was in dispensing fruit, vegetables, and fish among the 'Children of the Sun,' she was miserly with her livestock. It remained for the Spaniards to introduce cattle, pigs, goats, and chickens to Mexico.

From these came tough beef (subsequently ground, sliced thinly, or cut into chunks for pot roasts, stews, and moles); excellent pork (the outstanding favorite); and tender young kid (which, barbecued, is a big fiesta favorite).

The chickens — scrawny, rangy, and tough — run loose all over Mexico. They are kept for their occasional eggs and are in grave peril with each new fiesta. When cooked, they are invariably stewed into submission, and then served in a spicy mole, or disintegrated and distributed among the tacos, enchiladas, and tamales. In spite of this, the chicken is surprisingly good.

Whatever the meat, with the addition of vegetables and local herbs and spices, the women of rural Mexico perform wonders in its preparation.

The face of this woman reflects the philosophy contained in the words of another Zapotec, the revered Benito Juarez, ex-president of Mexico: 'Respect for the rights of others, this is peace.'

CHILE CON CARNE ESTILO TEJANO

1 pound lean beef, cubed
1 pound pork, cubed
1/4 cup oil
1 onion, chopped
2 garlic cloves, minced
2 cans (8-ounce) tomato sauce

2 cups water
4 T mild chile powder
2 T cocoa
2 t salt
2 t oregano
1 t cumin

106

Brown meat in hot oil; put it in a large pot for further cooking.

Saute onion and garlic in the same oil; add to the meat. Add all remaining ingredients and mix well.

Cover pan tightly and cook over low heat — about 1 1/2 hours — or until meat is tender.

For chile con carne with beans, add 4 cups of cooked Mexican beans to the pot and stir occasionally without breaking them.

Serve with tortillas.

CHILE CON CARNE A LA MEXICANA

2 pounds lean beef, cubed
3 T oil
1 onion, chopped
2 garlic cloves, minced
2 cups water
3 T mild chile powder

2 t oregano
1/2 t cumin
1/2 t salt
Freshly ground pepper to taste
1/4 cup pickled jalapeño chiles, minced

Brown meat in hot oil and put in a large pot. Saute onion and garlic in the same oil; add it to the meat. Add all remaining ingredients except the peppers.

Cover pot and cook over low heat — about 1 1/2 hours — or until the meat is tender.

Just before serving, add the hot peppers. These are really hot, and the full effect is not immediately noticeable — so be careful.

We found the people of rural Mexico, like this farmer from Michoacan, to be warm-hearted and responsive, very hard-working and competent. We were strongly impressed by their simple sense of personal dignity and honest self-respect.

ALBONDIGON

Sauce: 1 pint tomato juice   1/2 t salt   1/4 cup cider vinegar
1/2 cup orange juice   1/2 t oregano   1/4 onion

2 pounds ground chuck
1 garlic clove, minced
1/4 cup onion, chopped
Salt and pepper to taste
3 strips bacon
1 cooked carrot, sliced

1 pimento, cut into strips
3 hard-boiled eggs, halved
1/4 cup cooked parsley, chopped
1 piece aluminum foil 12 x 24 inches
2 bay leaves
1/4 cup green peas

109

For sauce: Liquify ingredients in blender for 2 minutes.

Flatten the meat on the foil to form a rectangular slab 1/4-inch thick. Top with remaining ingredients, except bay leaves.

Roll tightly, wrap in foil, and put in a large pot. Cover with cold water, add bay leaves, and bring to a boil. Simmer over medium heat 45 minutes.

Remove from water, cool completely. Slice and serve cold with sauce.

Traditionally served with hot tortillas, guacamole, and preserved fruit, this is a complete menu for a special day.

1 pound boneless lean beef, cubed
2 pieces marrowbone
1 large onion, chopped
1 garlic clove, minced
12 peppercorns
1 chicken, cut into sections
1/2 pound ham, cubed
1/2 pound chorizo, rolled into small balls
2 t salt
4 large carrots, cut into 1-inch lengths
1 cup string beans, cut into sections
1 cup whole-kernel corn
4 zucchini, unpeeled, cut into 1-inch pieces

4 boiling potatoes
2 T oil
2 T butter
3 large firm bananas
2 pounds canned garbanzo beans, drained
2 avocados, diced
1/3 cup cilantro, chopped (or parsley)

Put beef, marrowbone, onion, garlic, and peppercorns in a large pot; cover with water, and boil slowly for 45 minutes.

Add chicken, ham, chorizo, salt, and water, if needed, to keep the meat covered. Bring to the boil, then simmer slowly 25 minutes. Add carrots and string beans. Simmer 15 minutes more, then add corn and squash. Cook 5 minutes more.

While meat is cooking boil the potatoes. Then peel, slice, and fry them in hot butter and oil. Brown both sides, and keep warm in a covered casserole.

Slice the bananas diagonally and fry them in the same pan until both sides are slightly browned. Place in casserole with potatoes.

Drain broth from the meat for soup and gravy — adding water and bouillon cubes, if necessary, to make up 12 cups. Put the meat and vegetables in another casserole to keep warm.

For gravy, thicken 2 cups broth with 2 T cornstarch.

For soup, add garbanzos to remaining broth, boil 5 minutes, pour into bowls and garnish with avocado and cilantro.

Refugio Masqueda Mercedes Chavez
makes charcoal from the
hardwood he gathers in the
hills above Guanajuato,
then hauls it down by burro
to sell in the towns.
His strongly Spanish features are
evidence of the harshness of
the occupation that
followed the Conquest of Mexico.

BISTEC ENROLLADO

Rolled Sirloin Strips
Serves 4

1 pound sirloin steak, sliced thinly
Sliced bacon (1 per piece of meat)
Chopped parsley
Oil for frying

Garnish: 3 red potatoes, sliced
          4 carrots, sliced
          1 cup water
          1/4 t salt
          2 T oil
Cook ingredients over low heat
10 minutes - or until tender.

Sauce: 1 large slice of onion
       1 garlic clove
       1/2 t salt
       4 whole cloves
       1/4 t cinnamon
       1/2 t sugar
       1 pound canned tomatoes
Liquify ingredients in blender.

113

Roll each slice of sirloin around a strip of bacon and 1 T parsley. Fasten with toothpicks. Brown in hot oil. Cover with sauce and simmer 45 minutes, or until meat is tender.   Serve with potatoes and carrots.

The Aztecs often dug deep holes, lined the edges with long maguey leaves standing on end, filled the cavity part way with large porous rocks, and built rip-roaring fires in the pit. When the coals were glowing, the Indians lowered large animals (and occasionally neighbors) onto them, folded the leaves over, covered this with straw petates and mud, and waited. The results were always — delicious!

The meat usually went into the hole whole — literally from chin to tail, or 'barba a cola.' And that's how the barbacoa got its name.

Meanwhile, in that vast territory to the north (later claimed as the great American Southwest), the ground was hard, the mud scarce, and the maguey leaves even scarcer. There they just tossed the neighbor's steer, lamb, or kid onto the open fire. Later called a 'barbecue,' it's just not the same.

For a reasonable substitute for the old-fashioned Indian style, try this:

1 leg of lamb: Roast, uncovered, in a 200° oven for 8 hours.

3 cups broth (add water to drippings)
1 small onion, chopped
2 T oil
1/2 cup rice
2 large carrots, sliced

2 T cilantro, chopped (or parsley)
2 boiling potatoes, sliced
2 canned chipotle chiles, minced
    or 2 jalapeño chiles +
    2 T smoked barbecue sauce

Saute onion in hot oil. Add rice; fry 3 minutes. Add the remaining ingredients. Add 2 cups of broth. Cover pan tightly with a lid, and cook over medium heat for 30 minutes.

Serve with the barbecued lamb along with the remainder of the broth thickened with 1 T cornstarch.

Josefina, the wife and helper of the charcoal maker, has the tremendous endurance and character of the women of rural Mexico.

CHULETAS DE CERDO A LA MORELIA

We thank Senora Maria Luisa Carillo de Padilla, manager of Hotel Acueducto in Morelia, for this excellent recipe.

4 thick loin pork chops
Salt and pepper to taste
1 T olive oil
1/2 onion, chopped
1 garlic clove, minced

1/2 t mild chile powder
1 pinch oregano
1 pinch cumin
1 cup water
1 T dry vermouth

117

Season chops with salt and pepper. Fry in hot oil until nicely browned. Remove from pan.

Saute onion and garlic, adding a little more oil if needed. Stir in chile powder, oregano, cumin, and water.

Return chops to pan, spoon sauce over them, cover pan, and let simmer for 15 minutes. Stir in vermouth just before serving.

Close by the Copper Canyon country of the high Sierra Tarahumara is the small lumbering town of Creel. In addition to the rustic Hotel Nuevo there once was an excellent small restaurant. To its amiable and long gone artist-chef, Fidel Carillo, we owe this recipe as well as several others in this book.

118

4 pounds lean pork, boneless
1/2 cup prepared mustard
1 can (6-ounce) tomato puree
3 garlic cloves, minced
1 cup onion, chopped
2/3 cup olive oil
2/3 cup water
1 cup white wine
1 bay leaf
2 T cornstarch mixed with 4 T water

Rub the meat with mustard, and set it in a large pot. Add remaining ingredients except cornstarch. Cook, tightly covered, for 3 hours. Remove meat, cool slightly, and slice.

Bring gravy to boil, add cornstarch mixture, stirring constantly. Return meat to gravy, and reheat.

Serve with cooked green peas.

Jose Arrendondo Aranda lives with his son in a shallow cave and guards a few small silver mines near Guanajuato. At one time mines of this area produced over half of the world's silver, but the flow has since dwindled to a trickle.

LOMO DE CERDO EN SALSA VERDE

Pork Loin in Green Sauce
Serves 8

4 pounds lean pork, boneless
1 onion, chopped
1 bay leaf
1/8 t marjoram
1/8 t thyme
2 t salt

Sauce: 1 onion, quartered
1 garlic clove
1 cup tomatillos (or green tomato relish)
1 large tomato, peeled and quartered
3 canned green chiles
2 T cooking oil
2 T cilantro, chopped (or parsley)
1 cup broth from meat
Salt and pepper to taste

121

Cover meat with cold water, Add onion, bay leaf, marjoram, and thyme. Cook, covered, 3 hours. Add salt after 1 1/2 hours.

Puree onion, garlic, tomatillos, tomato, and chiles. Fry paste in hot oil for 5 minutes. Stir in cilantro and broth; salt and pepper to taste.

Slice the meat, add it to the sauce, and simmer 30 minutes.

Serve with hot rice or boiled potatoes.

Credited to divine inspiration in the Convent of Santa Rosa of 16th-century Puebla, this was probably a royal fiesta dish pre-dating the Conquest. The sauce alone contained 29 ingredients and took more than a day to prepare.

Today, the spices and seasonings are obtainable already blended in Mole Poblano pastes and powders, and satisfactorily simulated in the modified and excellent recipe given below.

122

4 pounds chicken breasts, halved
Oil for frying
2 garlic cloves, minced
1 medium onion, sliced
1 small tortilla, cut into strips
1/4 cup raisins
1/4 cup blanched almonds
1 T sesame seeds
1 T cilantro (or parsley)

1/2 pound tomatoes, peeled and seeded
2 T olive oil
7 T mild chile powder
1/4 t each: cumin, cloves, cinnamon, coriander seeds, anise, sugar
3/4 t salt
1 ounce unsweetened chocolate, melted
3 cups chicken broth

Brown the chicken on all sides in hot oil; set aside.

Blend the next 8 ingredients to a smooth paste. Add chile powder, seasonings, and melted chocolate.

Heat olive oil in a large frying pan; fry the above sauce 5 minutes, lowering the heat as soon as sauce is in the pan; stir to prevent burning.

Stir in the broth, add chicken, cover pan; simmer over low heat 30 minutes.

Serve with a green salad, Mexican rice, and hot tortillas.

The countenance of this Mixtec tells something of the life in the Upper Mixteca. She had been watching us from a distance for some time and, despite her great reserve, consented to being photographed with her son.

POLLO EN JUGO DE NARANJA

1/2 cup flour
1 t salt
1/4 t pepper
4 whole chicken breasts, halved
1/4 cup olive oil
1/2 onion, chopped
2 garlic cloves, minced
1/2 cup almonds, slivered

1 cup orange juice
1/2 cup crushed pineapple, drained
1/4 cup raisins
2 T sugar
1/2 t cinnamon
1/8 t ground cloves
1 cup white wine

Mix flour, salt and pepper, and use to coat chicken. Brown chicken in hot oil and then arrange in casserole.

Saute onion, garlic, and almonds in the same oil; add remaining ingredients EXCEPT wine, and pour this sauce over chicken.

Cover casserole and bake in 325° oven for 30 minutes.

Uncover casserole, turn chicken, pour wine overall. Increase temperature to 350° and bake for 15 minutes more. Serve with steamed rice.

Here is a Mexican version of a dish popular throughout Latin-America.

6 strips bacon, halved
1/2 onion, chopped
1 garlic clove, minced
1/4 cup oil
1 fryer chicken, sectioned
1 cup rice

2 fresh tomatoes, peeled and chopped
1/4 t cumin
1 1/2 cups chicken broth
Salt and pepper to taste
1 cup cooked green peas

126

Fry bacon lightly; remove from pan. Saute onion and garlic in bacon fat; set aside. Add oil to the bacon fat and brown the chicken; set chicken aside and fry the rice in the same pan for 3 minutes.

Stir in the tomatoes and cumin; add the chicken, bacon, and sauteed onion and garlic to the pan. Sprinkle with salt and pepper, and pour broth overall.

Cover pan tightly and simmer for 30 minutes without lifting the lid. When done stir in the cooked green peas, and serve.

Though chorizo can be purchased in many supermarkets, here is a superb mix that you can make and store in the refrigerator for several weeks.

1/2 pound ground beef
1/2 pound pork sausage
1/2 onion, chopped
2 garlic cloves, minced
2 T mild chile powder
3 T vinegar

1/4 t pepper
1/2 t cinnamon
1/4 t cloves
1 t oregano
1 t salt
1 recipe Mexican Beans (see page 78)

Mix all ingredients and refrigerate 4 hours before using.
Make Mexican Beans recipe separately.
Shape sausage into balls; brown well in a dry frying pan. Drain off fat.
Mix sausage with cooked beans and simmer for 30 minutes.

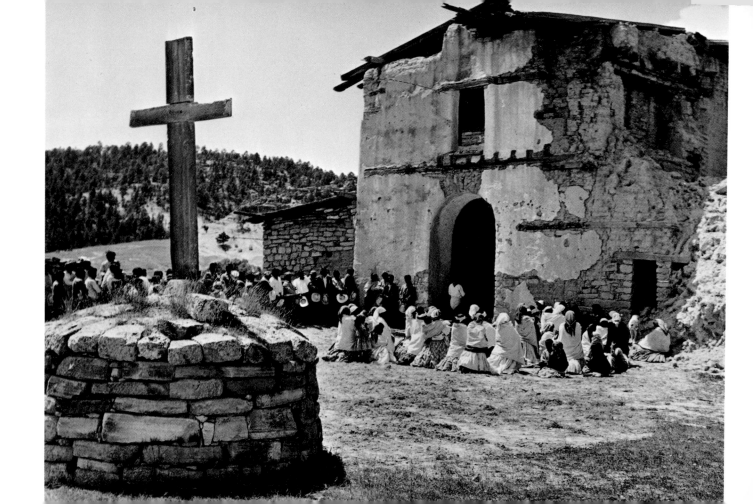

There were turkeys, ducks, smaller fowl, and turtles in pre-Conquest Mexico. But in colonial Mexico, chickens from Spain supplied the eggs.

Hard-boiled, soft-boiled, and poached; fried, scrambled, and in omelettes — and always accompanied by warm tortillas, refried beans, and coffee of sorts — chicken eggs quickly became the mainstay of Mexican breakfasts.

Beyond this, with concentration of interest on culinary arts in the royal courts of Europe, as well as in the palaces and mansions of colonial Mexico during the 17th and 18th centuries, and with the new supply of New World fruits and legumes, wonderful new dishes developed.

The offerings in the following pages are ideal for a lazy brunch or breakfast.

The timorous Tarahumaras only slip down from their primitive caves and huts to attend Mass, watch a Baptism or an occasional marriage ceremony, or seek medicine or counsel from the padre on his monthly visit. He is the only outsider they trust.

HUEVOS MALAGUEÑA

This easy and elegant dish can be put together ahead of time and slipped into the oven later. Served with fresh fruit salad, hot rolls, and cafe con leche (half hot milk, half strong coffee), it is the mainstay for an excellent party brunch.

1 can tomato soup
1/2 cup tomato, peeled, seeded
1/4 cup water
1/4 t sweet basil
Salt and pepper to taste

3 ounces shrimp, cooked
12 asparagus spears, canned
8 stuffed Spanish olives, sliced
8 eggs

130

Mix the soup, tomato, water, basil, salt and pepper. Divide half the mixture between 4 individual baking dishes.

Arrange the shrimp, asparagus, and olives in the dishes.

Break 2 eggs carefully into each dish, cover with the remaining sauce, and bake in 350° oven for 20 minutes, or to individual taste.

HUEVOS YUCATECOS

2 bananas

2 T butter

8 tortillas

Oil for frying

8 eggs

1 cup refried beans, warmed

1 cup cooked ham, chopped

1/3 cup Parmesan cheese, grated

2/3 cup peas, cooked

Sauce: 3 T onion, chopped with 2 garlic cloves

1/4 cup olive oil

3 tomatoes, peeled and chopped

1 cup tomato sauce

1/3 cup canned green chiles, chopped

1/2 t sugar

1/2 t vinegar

1 bay leaf

1 cup chicken broth

Sauce: Saute onion and garlic in hot oil. Stir in tomatoes and tomato sauce. Fry for 5 minutes. Add remaining ingredients; simmer 5 minutes.

Slice bananas lengthwise, then in halves; fry in butter until browned.

Fry tortillas in hot oil. Drain on paper towels. Fry eggs according to taste.

Place 2 tortillas on a plate, spread with beans, top with 2 eggs, peas, and ham. Pour sauce overall, sprinkle with cheese, and garnish with fried bananas.

Hermina's most cherished possession, her harmonica, provides music for her classmates as they dance the pascoles and matachines. It also provides companionship on the lonely days with the sheep and goats in the hills, as well as comfort by the coals of a fire in a cave at night.

HUEVOS Y CHILAQUILES

1/2 cup onion, minced
1/3 cup butter
4 tortillas, cut into 1-inch squares
1/4 cup mild chile powder
8 eggs, slightly beaten
1/4 cup canned green chiles, chopped
Salt and pepper to taste
1/4 cup Parmesan cheese, grated
2 T parsley, chopped

Saute onion in heated butter. Add tortillas and chile powder, stirring well to coat tortillas with powder, and cook until browned.

Add eggs, green chiles, salt and pepper; scramble.

Sprinkle with Parmesan cheese and parsley.

HUEVOS REVUELTOS A LA MEXICANA   Scrambled Eggs Mexican Style
Serves 4

2 T butter
8 eggs
2 T cream
2 small tomatoes, peeled, chopped
2 T canned green chiles, chopped
2 T onion, chopped
2 T parsley, chopped
2/3 cup mild Cheddar cheese, cubed
Salt and pepper

134

Melt butter in frying pan.

Beat eggs with the cream, and pour into pan. When eggs have set slightly add other ingredients, and scramble.

Serve with juice, refried beans, hot rolls, and cafe con leche (half strong coffee, half hot milk, with sugar to taste).

HUEVOS RANCHEROS

Huevos rancheros are a standard item all over Mexico — yet we've never had them cooked the same way twice. Here is our favorite recipe.

1 cup onion, chopped
1 garlic clove, minced
3 T butter
3 cups tomatoes, peeled and chopped
1 1/2 T salsa Jalapeña

Salt and pepper to taste
8 tortillas
Oil for frying
8 fried eggs

135

Saute onions and garlic in butter.
Add tomatoes and relish; simmer 1/2 hour. Season to taste.
Fry tortillas in hot oil and drain on paper towels.
Place 2 tortillas on each warmed plate, top with 2 eggs, cover with sauce.
Serve with extra tortillas.

Indian children at the Tarahumara Mission Boarding School near Creel quickly overcome their traditional shyness. They learn Spanish and practical subjects in a program to increase the chances of survival of this beautiful, primitive race.

HUEVOS Y CHORIZO

For a hearty breakfast, serve with fruit, refried beans, sweet rolls, and coffee.

1 cup chorizo sausage (see page 127)
8 eggs, slightly beaten
1/2 cup green onions, chopped
NO OIL OR SEASONINGS

Put chorizo in a cool frying pan; turn heat to medium; fry until done.
Add beaten eggs and onions; scramble gently with chorizo, and serve.

Enhance the exotic: Serve with chilled sliced mangoes and cafe de olla (strong black coffee with brown sugar and cinnamon).

Sauce: 2 small avocados, mashed
1 tomato, peeled and chopped
1/4 cup onion, minced
2 t cilantro, minced (or parsley)
Salt and pepper to taste

1 cup ground beef
Oil for frying
1/4 cup onion, minced
1/8 t thyme
1/4 t oregano
2 t mild chile powder
1/3 cup sour cream

8 tortillas
Oil for frying
8 eggs
1/3 cup Parmesan cheese

For sauce: Mix first 5 ingredients well.

Brown meat in a little oil, add onion and seasonings, and simmer until onion is soft. Stir in sour cream, and keep warm.

Fry tortillas lightly in hot oil and drain on paper towel. Place 2 tortillas on each plate. Top with the meat, avocado mix, 2 fried eggs, and a sprinkling of cheese.

All the common fruits and most of the exotic tropical varieties — sun-ripened, extra-large, sweet and juicy — abundantly displayed in the markets; or chilled and peeled, sprinkled with lemon, ready for eating from the colorful small stands in the streets: These supply Mexico's favorite desserts.

In addition there are the candied squashes of the ancients, the rolls of ground nuts bonded with honey, sweet tamales, that are always served with hot sugarless chocolate.

With the introduction of milk, chicken eggs, and sugar, more desserts were added in the 17th century . . . mostly by the good nuns of Puebla. Of these a custard, flan, has become and has remained the national dessert.

These children, from widely scattered huts in the upper Mixteca, are taught by a local teacher who received four years of secondary education under a government program for rural teachers, then returned home - as she had promised - to teach.

By popular acclaim from border to border and sea to sea, this Flan Supreme is the national dessert.

Sauce: 1 cup sugar

For sauce: Put sugar in pan and cook over low heat, stirring until melted and golden brown. Pour into mold and spread over the sides. This will harden, but will soften again when flan is cooking.

Pudding: 1 quart milk or half-and-half
3/4 cup sugar
1/8 t salt
1 t vanilla
6 large eggs, well beaten

For pudding: Mix the milk, sugar, and salt; boil vigorously for 10 minutes. Add mixture to the eggs, a little at a time, beating constantly. Continue beating for 3 minutes while mixture cools. Stir in vanilla. Set oven at 300°.

Pour mixture into mold and cook in waterbath (large pan half filled with hot water) 1 1/2 hours, or until knife inserted in flan comes out clean.

Chill in refrigerator. Unmold on dish with a raised edge, to hold sauce.

Elegant touch: Pour brandy or rum over flan and light it just before serving.

Like little girls the world over, these three sisters from the Aztec village of Milpa Alta, near Mexico City, cherish the dolls they received on Three Kings Day, the traditional day for presents in Mexico.

These are good hot or cold - any time: as the finishing touch to a brunch, as an afternoon treat, or for an after-dinner dessert.

4 firm bananas
4 T lemon juice
8 T brown sugar
1/2 cup whipping cream
8 maraschino cherries, chopped

Wash bananas, since they are to be cooked in the peel.

Loosen one narrow strip of peeling on each banana. Carefully take out the banana, dip in lemon juice, roll in brown sugar, and return to peel.

Wrap bananas tightly with foil and bake in 375° oven for 1/2 hour.

Remove bananas from peel; serve in banana-split dishes topped with whipped cream and cherries.

FLAN DE ALMENDRA

Almond Flan
Serves 8

1 quart milk
1 1/3 cups sugar
1 1/2 ounces almonds, blanched and ground
8 egg whites, beaten until peaks form

146

Combine milk, sugar, and almonds in a saucepan. Boil for 5 minutes, stirring constantly. Remove from heat and let cool.

Fold in egg whites. Pour into a well-greased mold and bake in waterbath (large pan half filled with hot water) in a 300° oven about 1 hour, or until a knife inserted in center comes out clean.

Cool completely.

Turn out on a serving plate and serve with cajete sauce (following page), or if you are in a hurry, use sauce on page 142.

The preparation time (1 1/2 hours) is worth the results. Not only is cajete a perfect companion for custard, it is excellent with ice cream. You can make larger quantities if you wish, as this sauce keeps well in a covered container.

1 quart milk
1 1/4 cups sugar
1 t baking soda dissolved in 1/4 cup water

In a large, deep saucepan, combine milk and sugar. Bring to a boil over low heat, stirring constantly.

Slowly add only the water from the baking soda (discarding the solids), and be prepared to lift the pan off the fire, as the mixture will rise considerably, and fast. After it subsides, return pan to low heat. (Too much heat will make it rise.)

Continue simmering gently, stirring constantly until mixture turns thick and brown, and the bottom of the pan can be seen in the wake of the spoon, about 1 1/2 hours.

Using her rebozo to help support her little brother, just as her mother does, and with an air of considerable practice and competence, this young Zapotec girl fulfills the role of bigger sisters all over Mexico.

PLATANOS FRITOS

During fiestas bananas cooked this way are sold from hand carts and stalls all over Mexico, and eaten on the spot.

4 large bananas, peeled and cut lengthwise
4 T butter
1 cup brown sugar
Juice of 2 oranges
Rind of 1 orange, grated
1/2 cup sour cream
1/2 cup powdered sugar

Fry bananas in melted butter 1 minute on each side.
Mix sugar, orange juice and rind; pour over the bananas.
Simmer until tender — about 15 minutes. Turn bananas and spoon syrup over them while cooking.
Serve warm with sauce made of equal parts sour cream and powdered sugar.

By using sweetened condensed milk and a pressure cooker, the cooking time for this outstanding dessert is reduced from the customary 2 hours to 15 minutes.

Sauce: 1/2 cup sugar

For sauce: Put the sugar in a pan and cook over low heat, stirring constantly until melted and golden brown. Pour into the mold and spread all around the sides. This will harden, but will soften again when the flan is cooking.

Pudding: 4 eggs
          1 can sweetened condensed milk
          1 cup water
          1 t vanilla

For pudding: Beat eggs 1 minute, add other ingredients, mix well. Pour into mold, cover, and place in pressure cooker on rack over 1 cup water. Cook under pressure for 10 minutes. Remove cooker to cool place while pressure drops.

As soon as you can, remove mold, let it cool further; then refrigerate.

For serving: Turn flan out onto a plate with a raised edge to contain the caramel sauce.

Zenon was sickly as a baby
and constantly pursued
by a witch which
sometimes took the
form of a small black dog,
his parents believe.
Today he is sturdy,
stolid, and always insists
on taking care of himself.

BUDIN DE ARROZ

1 cup water
1 pinch salt
1 piece lemon peel
1 cup rice
1 quart milk

2 egg yolks, beaten in 1/4 cup of the milk
1 cup sugar
1/2 cup raisins
Cinnamon

Bring water to a boil. Add salt, lemon peel, and rice, and boil slowly, stirring occasionally until water is absorbed.

Add milk and continue boiling until pudding becomes thick and rice is soft. Stir frequently to prevent burning.

Stir in beaten egg yolks, sugar, and raisins. Bring to a boil.

Pour into 2-quart greased mold. Chill thoroughly.

Serve sprinkled with cinnamon. Top with whipped cream, rompope, or chilled berries, if desired.

153

MERENGUES

Meringues are sold in bakeries all over Mexico. They are particularly delicious filled with pineapple custard, topped with whipped cream, cherries, and nuts.

2 egg whites
1/2 cup sugar
1/8 t salt

1/4 t cream of tartar
1/2 t vanilla

154

Beat egg whites until foamy.

Gradually add sugar, salt, cream of tartar, and vanilla, beating at high speed until stiff.

Drop mixture by large spoonsful on ungreased cookie sheet or foil. Indent each, like a nest, and bake in 250° oven until dry (45 minutes or more).

Store in an air-tight container. If meringues should soften, simply heat them in a slow oven a few minutes, until crisp again.

Serve filled with pineapple custard (following page).

NATILLA DE PIÑA

4 egg yolks, well beaten
2 cups milk
2 T cornstarch dissolved in 4 T of the milk
4 T sugar
1 cup canned pineapple, drained and pureed
1/2 t pineapple flavoring

155

Mix egg yolks, milk, cornstarch, and sugar. Cook over low heat (or in double boiler) stirring constantly, until mixture thickens and coats the spoon.

Remove from heat. Stir in pineapple and flavoring. Chill before filling meringues.

With flowers picked that morning, two friends make their way to church with flowers for the altar of the Blessed Virgin, the village's patron saint.

ROMPOPE

In Mexico this is served with cookies as a late afternoon refreshment, or in sherry glasses as an after-dinner drink. It is also used as a dessert sauce for jellos, puddings, and flans. It is also an excellent base for egg nog!

1 quart milk	1 t vanilla
1 cup sugar	1 cup rum or brandy
8 egg yolks	

Boil milk and sugar over low heat for 10 minutes, stirring constantly. Remove from fire and cool 5 minutes, stirring to prevent skin from forming.

Beat egg yolks well and stir into the milk. Return mixture to the fire and cook until it coats the spoon well.

Immediately transfer mixture to a bowl set in cold water, stirring occasionally during first few minutes of cooling.

Stir in vanilla and rum (or brandy). Bottle before refrigerating.

NATILLA DE CARRILLO

2 egg yolks, slightly beaten
1 T cornstarch, dissolved in 2 T milk
2 cups milk
1/2 cup sugar
1/4 t cinnamon
1 t vanilla

4 thick slices pound cake
1 cup heavy cream whipped with
   3 T sugar and 1/2 t vanilla
2 ounces rum
Red and green maraschino cherries

158

Mix egg yolks, cornstarch, milk, sugar, and cinnamon in small saucepan. Cook over low heat, stirring constantly, until mixture thickens and coats the spoon. Add vanilla and cool.

Spread pound cake slices on a plate, and soak with rum.

Crumble 2 slices in bottom of mold (preferably cake pan with loose sides). Top with half of the custard, the rest of the pound cake, and remaining custard.

Chill in refrigerator for at least 1 hour. Unmold, cover with whipped cream, decorate with cherries, and serve.

CALABAZA ENMIELADA

Candied Squash
Serves 6

Although listed here as a dessert, this candied squash with milk poured over it is often served at breakfast in Mexico.

2 cups dark brown sugar
1 cup water
2 pounds banana squash

Garnish: Whipped cream
        Chopped nuts

Mix sugar and water in saucepan.

Peel squash. Cut it into 3-inch squares. Add to the sugar mixture. Cover pan, and cook over low heat until squash is tender.

Uncover pan and continue cooking until the syrup is thick, stirring frequently to prevent burning. Chill before serving topped with whipped cream and nuts.

Although the tortilla is the basic food of the masses, great quantities of mouth-watering items are baked in the villages, towns, and cities of Mexico — using methods and recipes imported from Spain.

For 100 years following Independence, as Mexico boycotted everything that was Spanish, French bakeries blossomed in the principal cities, catering to the fantasies and exuberances of the 'upper strata.'

Then, the Revolution put an end to the upper classes — and to the French pastries as well. Overnight, bakery items became simple and Spanish again — Spanish because this was the only other tradition the bakers knew.

Only recently is the pattern again being modified, as better ovens, package mixes, and modern customs take hold.

A day-long pageant - the Plume Dance of Teotitlan - is begun with a procession, with each villager responding to his lost traditions. It was here, according to legend, that the Zapotec race began.

BUÑUELOS

Buñuelos are a special Christmas tradition. In Oaxaca, the emptied bowls are smashed on the ground for good luck. By midnight the streets are ankle-deep in broken crockery.

Syrup: 2 cups dark brown sugar
1 cup water
1 stick cinnamon
Boil ingredients 1/2 hour.

1/4 cup water
1/4 t anise seeds
2 cups flour
1/2 t salt
1/2 t baking powder
1 T sugar

1 egg, slightly beaten
1/4 cup milk
2 T shortening, melted

Boil water with anise seeds; set aside to cool; strain, reserving water.

Sift dry ingredients, stir in eggs, milk, and anise water. Add melted shortening and mix well.

Knead dough on floured board for 3 minutes. Roll pieces the size of walnuts into balls, and let stand covered with cloth 30 minutes. Roll out on board to very thin circles.

Fry in hot oil on both sides until golden brown. Drain on paper towels. Dip bunelos in hot syrup and serve in soup bowls with extra syrup.

Benjamin Martinez portrays Cortez in the Pageant of the Plume Dance honoring Teotitlan's patron saint. This pageant has been produced continuously for 400 years.

A Mexican favorite, this pound cake will freeze well.

1 cup butter	1/4 t almond extract
1 2/3 cups sugar	2 cups cake flour
5 large eggs	1/2 t salt
1 1/2 T lemon juice	

Cream butter and sugar well. Add eggs, one at a time, beating after each addition. Add lemon juice and almond extract; beat mixture. Sift in flour and salt. Beat mixture well and pour into a paper-lined loaf pan.

Bake in 325° oven until a toothpick inserted in the cake comes out clean (about 1 hour and 20 minutes).

Let cake cool in pan 5 minutes, then lift it out to finish cooling on cake rack.

1/2 cup butter	2 cups carrots, freshly shredded
1 cup sugar	2 cups blanched almonds, ground (measure after grinding)
5 egg yolks	1 lemon, juice and rind
1/2 cup flour	2 T rum
1 t baking powder	5 egg whites, beaten until stiff peaks form

166

Thoroughly grease and flour an angel-cake pan.

Cream butter and sugar; add yolks one at a time, beating well after each addition. Add flour sifted with baking powder, then carrots, almonds, lemon rind, lemon juice, and rum. Mix well, and fold in egg whites. Pour mixture into cake pan.

Bake in 350° oven 1 hour 20 minutes or until inserted knife comes out clean. Then cool in mold for 20 minutes. Turn onto a plate and sprinkle with powdered sugar.

Serve warm or cold.

TORTA DE GARBANZO

Here's a pudding cake: heavy and moist, nourishing and healthful!

2 pounds canned garbanzo beans, drained
1/2 cup evaporated milk
6 egg yolks
1 1/2 cups sugar

1/4 t salt
1/4 t cinnamon
4 egg whites, beaten until peaks form
1 cup raisins

Puree garbanzos and milk in blender, a little at a time.

Beat egg yolks with sugar, salt, and cinnamon until thick; fold into garbanzos, blending well.

Fold in the beaten egg whites and the raisins.

Grease an angel-cake pan well, dust with flour, and pour batter into the pan.

Bake in 350° oven 1 hour 20 minutes, or until a toothpick inserted in the center comes out clean. Cool 20 minutes in pan, unmold, and sprinkle with powdered sugar. Chill before serving.

Teotitlan's many religious processions are participated in by the entire community, with the youngest member taking an early interest in becoming members of the band.

PASTELITOS DE BODA

These small cakes (or cookies), similar to our 'melt-aways,' are sold for all occasions all over Mexico, and always served with hot chocolate.

3/4 cup shortening	2 cups sifted flour
1/2 cup powdered sugar	1 cup walnuts, finely chopped
2 t vanilla	1/4 cup heavy cream

Cream shortening with sugar, then add vanilla. Beat in flour and nuts. Add cream; knead lightly; shape into a 2 1/2-inch in diameter roll; wrap in wax paper. Chill in refrigerator for several hours.

Cut roll into 1/4-inch slices. Place on ungreased cookie sheets, and bake at 375° for 15 minutes.

Remove from cookie sheets, place on cooling rack, and generously sprinkle with powdered sugar while still hot.

A rich gold cake with coffee frosting, this is one of the most popular desserts in Mexico City.

1/2 pound butter

1 1/2 cups sugar

6 egg yolks, beaten until thick and light yellow

1/2 t vanilla

6 egg whites, beaten until stiff peaks form

2 cups sifted flour

1 1/2 t baking powder

1/2 t salt

170

Beat butter until fluffy; add sugar and beat well. Add yolks and vanilla. Beat thoroughly. Fold in egg whites, then flour sifted with baking powder and salt.

Line 2 round (9-inch) cake pans with waxed paper. Divide dough between the two, spreading it evenly. Bake in 325° oven about 50 minutes, or until a toothpick inserted comes out clean. Cool 10 minutes in pans, turn out on cake racks, and cool completely before frosting.

Frosting: 1/3 cup butter
1 pound powdered sugar, sifted
5 T canned milk
1 T instant coffee
1 t vanilla
1 cup apricot jam
1 Hershey candy bar

Cream butter; add sugar alternately with milk, beating well. Add coffee and vanilla; beat until fluffy.

Spread 1 layer with jam, add second layer, then frost. Decorate with curls shaved from candy bar.

The feelings of kinship and harmony which characterize many villages in rural Mexico are evident in the community fiestas in which everyone participates.

ALL THE CHILES used in this book are generally available in supermarkets and specialty shops. The fresh and dried forms produce the best dishes.

Anchos — large, mild dark red, sold dried.
Chipotle — medium-sized, red smoked, very hot; sold canned.
Pequines — pea-sized, red, very hot; sold dried, and as "crushed red peppers."
Green Chiles — large, green, mild Poblanos and Californias, sold fresh and canned.
Jalapeños — medium-sized, green, very hot; fresh and canned as "hot peppers." 173

In preparing dried chiles, wash, dry and place on foil 5 inches under broiler. Toast until puffy and soft. Put fresh green chiles on foil 3 inches under broiler and turn until skin is blistered on all sides, cool slightly and peel. Remove stems, seeds, and lateral veins.
KEEP HANDS AWAY FROM EYES AND WASH HANDS THOROUGHLY WITH SOAP AND COLD WATER IMMEDIATELY AFTERWARD.

INDICE

"The PEACE of GOD be with you."